How We Spent Our Time

Akron Series in Poetry

2004 AKRON POETRY PRIZE WINNER

AKRON SERIES IN POETRY
Elton Glaser, Editor

Barry Seiler, *The Waters of Forgetting*
Raeburn Miller, *The Comma After Love: Selected Poems of Raeburn Miller*
William Greenway, *How the Dead Bury the Dead*
Jon Davis, *Scrimmage of Appetite*
Anita Feng, *Internal Strategies*
Susan Yuzna, *Her Slender Dress*
Raeburn Miller, *The Collected Poems of Raeburn Miller*
Clare Rossini, *Winter Morning with Crow*
Barry Seiler, *Black Leaf*
William Greenway, *Simmer Dim*
Jeanne E. Clark, *Ohio Blue Tips*
Beckian Fritz Goldberg, *Never Be the Horse*
Marlys West, *Notes for a Late-Blooming Martyr*
Dennis Hinrichsen, *Detail from* The Garden of Earthly Delights
Susan Yuzna, *Pale Bird, Spouting Fire*
John Minczeski, *Circle Routes*
Barry Seiler, *Frozen Falls*
Elton Glaser and William Greenway, eds., *I Have My Own Song for It:*
       Modern Poems of Ohio
Melody Lacina, *Private Hunger*
George Bilgere, *The Good Kiss*
William Greenway, *Ascending Order*
Roger Mitchell, *Delicate Bait*
Lynn Powell, *The Zones of Paradise*
Dennis Hinrichsen, *Cage of Water*
Sharmila Voorakkara, *Fire Wheel*
Vern Rutsala, *How We Spent Our Time*

How We Spent Our Time

Poems by
Vern Rutsala

The University of Akron Press
Akron, Ohio

All inquiries and permission requests should be addressed to the Publisher,
The University of Akron Press, 374B Bierce Library, Akron, Ohio 44325-1703.

LIBRARY OF CONGRESS CATALOGING-IN-PUBLICATION DATA
Rutsala, Vern.
  How we spent our time / Vern Rutsala.-- 1st ed.
    p. cm. — (Akron series in poetry)
  ISBN 1-931968-28-4 (alk. paper)
  I. Title. II. Series.

PS3568.U83H69 2005
811´.54—DC22

                                    2005031553

The paper used in this publication meets the minimum requirements of American
National Standard for Information Sciences—Permanence of Paper for Printed Library
Materials, ANSI Z39.48–1984. ∞

ACKNOWLEDGMENTS
Thanks to the editors of the following periodicals in which these poems, sometimes in
somewhat different form, originally appeared.

The American Poetry Review: Making Lists; *Calapooya Collage*: Looking for Work,
Travelling One Way; *College English*: Moon Driving, Writing to the Past; *Colorado
State Review*: Remaking Yourself; *Crazyhorse*: Missing It; *Denver Quarterly*: Depart-
ing, Arriving . . . ; *Epoch*: Sleeping for a Year; *Fine Madness*: Learning to Draw; *Har-
vard Magazine*: Living Somewhere Else; *Hubbub*: Camping with Ecclesiastes, Driving
North; *The Hudson Review*: Talking to Strangers; *Indiana Review*: Owning Things;
The Journal: Killing Time; *The Laurel Review*: Getting and Spending; *Ohio Review*:
Disappearing; *Oregon English*: Keeping It Together; *Ploughshares*: Killing Flies in
Georgia; *Poetry*: Becoming American, Coming Home, Listening to a Russian Choir,
Taking Shelter; *Poetry East*: Learning Your Lesson; *Seneca Review*: Letting Things
Slide; *Sewanee Review*: Getting Out of the Army (as "Flying Free in Fifty-eight"),
Reclaiming the House; *Stand*: Going To England; *The Talking of Hands*: Taking the
Old Road; *Tar River Poetry*: Calling Up the Pain, Making a Living; *Telescope*: Dream-
ing of Journeys; *Wigwag*: Taking Pictures.

The author wishes to thank the Oregon Arts Commission for the Master's Fellowship
that helped him to complete this book. "Travelling One Way" was awarded the Car-
olyn Kizer Poetry Prize. "Looking for Work" received a merit award in an earlier Kizer
competition. "Going to England" was broadcast on *Poetry Now* on BBC3 in London.
"Listening to a Russian Choir" was awarded the Duncan Lawrie Prize by the Arvon
Foundation.

Contents

To Joan

Departing, Arriving . . .

Both go on in the terminal's cathedral
        hush—ceilings so high, voices trailing
               off into wisps in the milky air.
Families huddle on the vast carpet's dizzy
              patterns, trussed hopes gathered
     at their feet for the long journeys in air
and darkness. See them cry as they leave

and come home, those wrenchings that may
        end in disaster either way.
             This place is like a hospital.
We wait on and on while instruments
        beyond our control make decisions
     we live and die with. Our bags are X-rayed,
our bodies scanned for evidence against us—

any odd shape gets closer looks from
        cold-eyed pros. Something is born,
           something else dies in this imitation air.
You overhear: "I called and tried to calm her
        down" and "He's at peace now"
     and all your occasions for grief push
gurneys down the concourse—how the first

time you flew first class was the winter
        your father died. You remember that cold
           flight over chalky plains, the land's

frozen coma beneath you, the stewardess a kind
                of nurse giving you doses of bourbon
        that didn't work. You remember him
wheeled from surgery like baggage, false teeth out,

chin trembling terribly. And how your mother
                cupped his chin to draw the trembling off,
                        her own hand taking on the shaking,
that shaking now contagious and your place on earth
                trembling under you the way it still trembles.
        Now, waiting for a plane you relive all
that waiting—in departure lounge and dim ward—

those grainy hours of dread and longing, mouth
        turned leather with cigarettes.
                Our spirit, wispy as it is, dwells here,
maneuvering this vacant air, this site of disembodied
                voices where hope and loss lurk in the white
        courtesy telephones that never ring and we
wait for our lives to come back to us at Baggage Claim.

Looking for Work

Today the line at the soup kitchen
was longer than last week—winter
is coming—and I remember that
summer years ago I spent mornings
on a bench at Third and Salmon
reading the way a hungry man eats,
caught in the gap between two fears—
not finding a job and finding one.
Those fears made the words glow
with some extra meaning—I was reading
Lie Down in Darkness and I sank
lower each day into darkness,
the summer slipping away with each
click of the checkers the players
near me moved with such care.
But I couldn't move as if fastened
there reading the same sentence over
and over, lost in a kind of waking coma.
I remember the dusty taste of those
mornings among the old men sunning
their drunk-tank stubble and how I
couldn't walk the block and a half
to the employment office. I knew
nothing waited there but the clerk's
dry lips saying "sorry" or, worse,
offering something terrible, some
blacking factory where I would disappear

forever, eaten alive by America's
fierce indifference. And I was helpless,
holding the book like a life preserver,
knowing I was wholly useless with hands
unable to do anything worth a single
measly dime to anyone anywhere.

Getting and Spending

Remember the day we saw three childhoods
for sale, those other times whole families
seemed smelted down to odds and ends?
Abandoned wives and husbands loomed through
the scattered jumble on picnic tables.
Despite such sad hints we keep going
because we love the useless—among the faded
and the bent we may find a story
about all our lives—of hot acquisition,
of slow relinquishment. Some days, though,
we wonder about how many more chipped
vases we can stand to look at,
how many commemorative mugs with crazed
interiors swallowing the dregs
of some forgotten glory. But we go on
studying the battered golf bag with its
three rusty clubs, the embroidered
pillows for a lost fair
on Atlantis. Once we found sheet music
left so long in a piano bench
every note was flat.
And there are always those odd tools
for machines that lost their patents
ages ago along with nuts and bolts
vainly searching for their mates.
Behind the array, figures mill faintly
with mumbled stories we never quite
hear—words about fresh starts, something

about good riddance to flat tires
and footballs, knobby fruit bowls,
sunglasses blinded by one too many rose-
colored views. We scan books so cheap
they beg with their soft dog ears
to be read just once more and always
the postcards with illegible messages
from the grave or scrawled arrows
pointing to "ME!" We find gifts fit only
for enemies—pens gone dry, paddles
without canoes, canoes without paddles,
electric cords so frayed their only purpose
is to start fires. And all those toys
so old they would turn children's hands
to rust. Bambi ashtrays, temperance coasters—
"Cold Water Cold Water For Me!"—
samplers saying Home Sweet Home
from broken homes. We keep plowing through
weekend after weekend, fondling
whatnot and knickknack, trying
to puzzle meanings for the completely obscure—
pomander holder? Shoe tree for Sasquatch?
Aztec sacrificial urn? Such uselessness
keeps us going, looking for childhoods and love
and ghosts swirling lost in myopic mirrors,
locked in steamer trunks without keys.

Letting Things Slide

Those stand-ins for the usual turmoil
        inside our lives turn up without
            invitation, taunting us—
that leaking pipe, those cracked tiles,
            each a comment on our deep
        incompetence—the furnace smoking
or coughing to a halt, a rain gutter

falling off while we sleep or the toilet
        simply going on strike without
            warning. This is the thing about
owning they never tell you—it's called
            keeping track, it's called
        maintenance, careful people we hate
call it "monitoring". And we know we're

at fault—the stand-ins make that clear.
        Stains splash down walls like stigmata
            and a crack in plaster draws
a cartoon lightning bolt that hits us deep
            like an arthritic stab and we're
        helpless, crawling through the yellow
pages for the help we know will be too late.

We've let things slide, haven't monitored
        our surroundings in the same way we've
            let our lives get away from us—
our balanced checkbook approach to history

is a mess. And that was
another trick—we thought you were
just supposed to live your life, not keep

track of every minute like some frantic
scorekeeper. But we send out our
dim SOSs anyway and the trucks
rumble to a stop out front and the repair men
come in with toolkits full of
remedies—but their kits rattle, sounding
like they're full of a deeper brokenness

and we're sure we'll get more problem
than solution out of them.
And it's true—they never really
fix what's wrong. Or, worse, each repair
uncovers something new and bad
and costly, broadly hinting at some
homeowners' entropy sucking us down its

bankrupt junkyard abyss. And this gets all
mixed-up with being wrong and fears
of secret eyeless creatures gnawing
the foundations and the luggage we must
carry—our special toolkits of despair—
toward the final dark appointment
when the very last thing goes wrong for good.

Dreaming of Journeys

I dream of journeys repeatedly
—Roethke

Our nights move across great distance
and we travel hard
through confusion—luggage lost,
tickets turned to dust, the arrogance
of border guards. And over each journey
is the sense of escape
from some unnamed crime, some
deep deceit we can't remember
though everyone we meet seems to know.
At times we wander through
an enormous jerrybuilt house
as populous as Asia, room upon room,
a house without end or back door,
without any way out. And over all this
lies an ominous fog,
some insufficient knowledge of ourselves.
We never let on of course
as we move through rooms near hysteria,
never questioning though we know something dark
is following, some careless act we've forgotten
writes its warrants and polishes its badges.
But somehow we stay ahead
and know that if we keep moving
through these rooms like sampans
we'll be safe. And so far we have been safe
though each night we grow more exhausted

as travel among these people
grows more difficult—so many call for help,
so many need transfusions or money.
We stop briefly and give
whatever quick help we can—a cold
compress, a dollar—knowing our compassion
is a ruse, an effort to throw off
those who follow, an effort to clear
a place in the fog of our conscience and buy a little time
from our pursuers, proving how decent
and honorable we are,
but we know deep in these swirling rooms
that no proof will ever be enough
and that the jerrybuilt rooms
will go on and on forever.

Becoming American

The Yankees needed ditch diggers,
sandhogs, fodder for the wild
hunger of their mills and sent out
invitations with no RSVPs.
My people came then, dimly knowing
they had to cut away the baggage
of the selves they brought with them.
The cutting was strangely easy
as they gaped at clerks smoothing
harsh corners off their names,
docking final vowels like tails.
Distance helped the cutting, too—
the ocean roiling behind them
with all that danger and disease,
the old country already swallowed
by the horizon's bulging lead.
At most it was only a village,
a hut, the midden out back
all frozen in the endless winter
of the past. The new language
squeezed more color from that past,
making it shameful—starving winds
and nothingness. They tugged
the new words into their mouths
like odd-shaped and exotic food,
curiously spiced, hard to choke down.
They rolled its oddness on their
tongues, tried to suck the sense

from it and the new ran together
with the old like milk in coffee,
the color changing until the old
was mostly gone, half their lives
dropping off the edge of the world.
Though some—my grandmother, maybe
yours—spat out the venom of the new words
and hung suspended between the two
languages, citizens of neither until
they lost both. Most learned the tricks
of getting by—how to count their pay,
the names of tools. Later they
prayed their children would have
no accents, knowing how their own
stubborn tongues kept them alien
and laughable, singsong and brogue
impossible to scrape away.
And then the generations forgot
their way across the muddy wilderness—
threshing wheat, scraping coal
from the dark, laying ties, clearing
homesteads with their bare hands.
They clawed away all memories
of the Atlantic and finally reached
the third and fourth generations
where the crops turned ironic.
The old thought it was a kind
of madness. Everything that was so
expensively forgotten, the crumpled
sheets of the past now started singing
like a siren to the young and they

longed for all those lost places.
They wanted the amnesia reversed.
They wanted the erased words back
in their mouths. The destroyed huts,
every ditch and abandoned village
crooned to them, bright and dear
and hopelessly beyond their reach.

Going to England

Going back this time we feel we're
paying the Pilgrims'
debt. It seems too far, measured
in years, and we'll be forced
to travel the Atlantic's
huge troughs in the smallest boat
ever made. But first
we have to clear this continent,
unpopulate it east and scatter the pieces
of every town until they
disappear. Part of the bargain
is to dance the buffalo back
and heal all the deaths
at Wounded Knee.
The bargain is impossible, of course,
but tonight we try.
We imagine the wilderness back
and deed it to the first
inhabitants as long as the grass
grows. They laugh, sure we're drunk.
And, of course, we are—
getting to England needs a lot
of fuel—but we keep trying
to make the land forget
it ever had a name like
The New World. We do the best
we can with dreams, clearing
away the signs the way

you clear a dinner table, piece by piece,
then pick up the map
and shake the last stubborn crumbs away.
Late as it is, this seems to work
and we feel the buffalo
and all the murdered
wolves come back silently.
Dreaming hard we make a checklist:
Rivers, mountains, plains, trees,
and every animal, every fish,
every bird. By main force we
bring them back and every stream
runs clear and water vapor
rises to clouds that bring
down a clean sweet rain.
It's very late now and we feel
we've earned our buckskin
passports which carry us to England
flying, because in dreams
you can always fly.

Taking Pictures

We have far more souls than we can ever use,
or so the photographer says.
At dawn they rise with us—
that flicker in the belly, that tickle in our throats,
that little ache fiddling along our ribs.
They want out
and travel with us all day
until two P.M. when the photographer arrives
with all his fussy gear.
His hungry shutter bites off one, then another,
soul after soul pulled through
that voracious lens
like a scarf through a keyhole.
Then he leaves quickly
juggling his camera like a hot potato,
hot with all our souls.
But we have plenty—
a real surplus, he says—
and we don't even miss those he takes away.
The many we have left whisper inside us
their language of twinge and tic,
wriggling like tadpoles,
eager for the next sitting.

Writing to the Past

We don't want to hear from them
again. We don't need
those haunted postmarks, that
penmanship of death.
This is why we make our letters
dull, we want no answers,
and begin each one with weather,
listing highs and lows
or annual rainfall figures.
But statistics aren't enough—
we need good news, too.
There's nothing like it
to shut them up and make
them cry. Good news by god
will freeze their ink
and make their stamps
lick themselves to death.
And we end each time
with, "Well, better close now
and go cash that big check
(ha ha)." And so far
this strategy has worked
and we're nearly certain
we'll never hear from them again,
but just to make sure
we're making plans
to use the telephone
to keep them good and quiet.

Talking to Strangers

Mainly you keep your mouth shut,
mainly you listen to your mother's
ghost and never talk to them,
but there are nights when your whole
life story rolls out with reckless ease.
You never know when it may happen,
it comes like a fever when you travel.
In trains or planes, in the bars
of strange hotels, you give yourself
away and tell all the secrets you never
tell your friends. And strangers
obey the fairness rule and tell you
secrets, too. You nod and grin
at stories of their wives and bosses.
They nod and grin for you.
This is all part of the game—
if you talk you must listen
just as you must admire wallet
photos and business cards.
Blabbermouths become good listeners
on nights like this. Nothing is close
to the vest and your whole flimsy
life becomes fabulous and rich.
Here the art is all touch-up and airbrush,
all shading and good light, subtle
forgery, burnished cameo.
On these nights you want your story
to ride like contraband in the back

of someone's mind, foggy from
the night before. You want it
to glide over streets you'll never see
and worm its way into someone else's
dreams. And you know that
whatever you confess, no matter
how tall your tale gets, no matter
how much you embroider and lie,
it will never be held against you.

Living Somewhere Else

First here is simplicity—
your whole life packed
in a few bags, dross and ballast
left behind, stacks of bills
and memories, cancelled checks
and the blue ribbon faded
almost to white.

          Here in a stranger's
house everything reinvents itself,
even cracks in plaster, even
that worn spot on the carpet—
each grain of sand becomes
intricate with interest.

          This is
the second chance you never
thought you'd get, a life like
gauze, like spring, a life you've
chosen and somehow lost
the old familiars—albatross
and monkey with those sharp
fingers.

          Back there it was
ratchet, it was visegrip;
here it's butter and double cream.
Here you move lightly from
room to room and not
a single thing clings to you

with the hooks of guilt.
Here you even learn a new
vocabulary that you whisper
as you float:

> *et sequentia,*
cinnabar, sage, Eugenie,
coriander, landau, celandine . . .

Sleeping for a Year

At first it was like driving a rented car
All that fine upholstery
Those responsive pedals
That sense of legal trespass no one minds
Every signal waved me on every cop smiled
I drove fast toward the north
Toward a city that lay on hills with grace
Its jetties entering a bay with skill
The sky was clear
The air the air I breathed in childhood
I counted the stars
Then it was the solitary train ride
I heard the sounds of shunting shouts swinging lanterns
I was alone in the neat compartment
All my needs were met
We moved through mountains across lakes
Over old cities of invitation new cities of rest
It was dark the whole way
And then it was a boat train
And we flowed slowly on some sea
The accommodations were perfect
String quartets sang while I drank tea
Casinos gave me chips
They let me break the bank over and over
Dancers danced themselves to butter for my amusement
There were bars on every deck
This was a good sleep
So good I went on adding nights

Until it became routine
They tell me I was still the whole time
They tell me I smiled gently
The boat docked and I moved silently
Across a landscape like a lawn
The tiny cows were real
They stared at me with the eyes of mice
Small people waved at every crossing
There were inns and farm houses
I lived in a thatched cottage
I went to the pub every night
The stout tasted as good as it looked
I walked on the common
I spoke to dogs and children
There were other warm wet meetings under the bushes
I ate simple hearty dishes
I drank calmness with my tea
Feeling an ease within me like a warm stone
Like an extra heart
I slept this way for a year
It took no effort

Making a Living

I think my way
east.

    It's the Great Plains,
the Midwest which
call

    past the melodrama
of the Rockies, past Montana's
self-indulgent

        scenery.
The call is toward people,
all those strangers
dotted on the country's middle—
and the question is:
How do they live?
Tonight it seems impossible—
those little towns
support only dust
and sheds where farmers oil
their big machines
twice a year.

        How do the people
live in those towns
that dwindle
before your eyes?

        Are they paid
to stand on street corners
and vote Republican?

        Is gossip

a kind of piecework?
The stores
                and lunch counters
always seem empty
                        and even
at the taverns I see
only one or two cars.
                        Moving deeper
where population maps
darken
        I wonder what people do
in Davenport and Moline.
How do they stay alive
on those gray streets?
                        Do they
really take in each other's
washing, living out a bad
joke?
        What do they do, spoon feed
each other, rob Peter to pay
Paul?
        But where does Peter's
money come from?
                        Some skim
the cream, of course, fingers
in the pie
                but what of the others?
And where does the cream—
or the pie for that matter—
come from?
                        That man

in Moline who looks like
my crazy uncle—
how does he live?
That family by the tracks
in South Bend—
                    what do they do?
Where do their potatoes
come from? Who brings home
the bacon?
                Okay, you say they
live by the sweat of their brows—
but why?
                The whole map is damp
with their sweat.
And what does sweat
sell for anyway?
                    Amid the noise
of factories there is
a great idleness, in Detroit's
crowded bars
                    a great silence.
How do the people live?
How do they make a living?
I can't think myself farther
though Akron and Pittsburgh beckon.
There are too many streets,
too many corners
and I give up
                letting the man in Moline
change a tire, his buddy call a cab.

Owning Things

This new tree can't be our emblem—it looks
too sick, needles almost yellow.
And no matter how much
we fuss around with water and hoes
we know it's bound to die.
Yes, it's ours but we want no part of it,
want to disown it, wish it would just
pull loose and crawl away some night for good.
We know about possession,
its nine points prick our skin with these dry needles.
Yet the tree gets sicker and sicker
in the lawn corner where the soil is jinxed.
True, we don't try that hard
but other trees did well—a pear, a lilac
that's nearly up to the eaves, three maples
that just dropped in on some windy whim.
Maybe that's the key—we don't own
those trees, they just settled like squatters.
Maybe that suits the way we are—
preferring to be chosen
rather than choosing for ourselves.
Or maybe the other trees own us
and slyly turn the ones we buy into outcasts
that die quickly of shame.
Owning things is strange.
Owning owns us, making us worry
about sick trees saying something secret
and dark about our lives to the neighbors.

We think they're sure its needles
turn brittle and dry because of our attention—
our thumbs the opposite of green,
the thumbs of killers finally.
And the tree says: I belong to you, this is what owning means—
a kind of slow murder.
We know what will happen: Some night after a few drinks
we'll dig it up and sneak it away to some
secret burial out of sight.
But ownership, being what it is, we'll remember
this tree and on bad nights
the dryness of its dying will flicker
across our skin and we'll own up,
admitting it was our emblem after all
and that it owns us still.

Making Lists

Whatever sorrow howls in the cold wind we still
make our lists, our maps of tomorrow
giving direction, place, and time,
assuming morning, assuming sunrise.
And maybe our lists are what bring us
our nightly serving of regret, this fog around us
of the done and not done. Whatever the case
we know too much has happened
that can never change—hospital vigils, the ragged
mouths of grief—and that we live now
where accident has taken us.
Yet we have these memo pads, these datebooks,
these dog-eared lists scrawled with errands,
with *things to do,* aimed to still the heart
of accident and turn our days predictable
and safe. But so many things weren't done,
the invisible duty, the item lost
in a fold. And maybe it's the undone
that inhabits the night with regret. Or maybe
it's just that habit of mind, that crimping caution
that made us hang back in childhood,
never wanting to be chosen first, wanting the safety
of falling somewhere in the middle.
So much was expected of the first chosen—
home runs, shoestring catches, even
the spectacular whoosh of the swinging third strike.
Though we knew all the stats—more lists—
we wanted none of the heroics, that mystery

of the unplanned. We were content
with right field or second base, a single
now and then, a walk.
And now, surrounded by our lists
of the undone, exhausted by a hot night,
we long for the home run, the hot bat,
the clutch hit we shied away from so hard.
We long for these and even regret our longing,
the past a list of things we never did.
But in the heat we trace the morning's
spidery script and remember how it led us
through the day, how, in fact, it held
our cautious day together.
Without the list we knew we would have lost
the day completely or, worse, expected heroics
from ourselves, some grand gesture, some decisive move.
So now we turn again in our circles,
remembering how we learned to arm ourselves
with lists that let us travel the hours safely.
Armed with lists we knew we would survive at least
until the next appointment. We loved the ease
of *this* then *this* and next *this*, knowing we were
here, say, at item seven, safe, with many more to go.
It was a kind of nourishment that kept away
the starving anarchy of nothing and ourselves.
The lists were our itinerary, our future plotted
yet picaresque, without resolution or the end of things.
We were in control! True travellers
of our lives, knowing we always had things to do!
But, of course, it's caught up with us
which is why we now maunder about roads not taken,

missed dates in wind and rain, the diminished thing—
our lives stretching backward, sleepless with regret
for the act that withered itself undone
because it wasn't on the list.
This is why we back and fill and learn again
the humbling art of being chosen fourth or fifth,
batting sixth or seventh and shifted to left
against lefthanders. As the hot hours grow small
we drop our names even deeper in the lineup
and switch ourselves strategically
to avoid error and embarrassment, our humility
the same old fear, the lineup card the same list
as we plot every minute of tomorrow, trying
to milk every ounce of danger from every second,
protected only by the calluses of habit.

Taking Shelter

With all the power out the house became
a cave with the cold rounding our
shoulders down through generation
after generation until we crept
and hunkered around the fire,
afraid that winter would never end.
Shadows played on the walls with menace
and wonder. We couldn't begin to catch
their flickery meaning but knew
they meant nothing good for us.
They were breathing a new ice age
into our lungs, reclaiming the house
room by room. In our shallow sleep
we dreamed of summer, leaves
breaking through their sheaths of ice.
Would it ever come again?
Need danced with the shadows, and heat
and food became our only concerns.
The house shrank to the space around
the fire yet it grew strangely, too,
the bedrooms moving far away
into the hills, perched on icy crags
and filled with who knew what sabre
teeth, what mastodons of ice and night
pawed and snorted up there?
Shelter's meaning ricocheted among
the shadows as cold proffered its sly
gifts—lassitude and that voluptuous

pull toward the heart of zero. But we kept
the fire going all night as night
lengthened toward a dawn that was
no gift. Tempers shortened with the fuel
supply and we felt betrayed by our
flimsy shelter. It invited every
wind inside and seemed less than
paper. On the fourth day the lights
flickered tauntingly and then
stayed dark, much darker than
before. The gods of ice were toying
with us. We huddled, listened less
to the radio—it came from too
far away, some place of heat and light
far beyond our pocket Yukon.
The next day the lights flickered
again—another trick we thought—
but then came on with a brilliance
we had never seen. Summer squeezed into
the house through those tiny wires
and we cheered but were leery,
all faith in electricity gone for good.
And now, a winter later, any flicker
of a lamp winces those cold days back
and we tense, waiting for darkness
and ice to move in and set up their
frigid housekeeping and start our
climb back through time to that cave
we now know every house wants to be.

Coming Home

We thought we knew these sidewalk cracks
by heart but even they have changed
since we left, branching out,
inventing new wrinkles.
The yard has a new identity, too—some plants
dead, others simply gone, without leaving
forwarding addresses.
Inside, the knives and forks don't look the same
and feel wrong in our hands—
the design more extreme than we remember
and there's also been some subtle change in scale.
The touch of all our familiar things
is strange, surfaces feel foreign
as if we've smuggled back
some alien coating.
Or they had taken some Berlitz course
in oddness while we were gone.
Even the old companions—tables, chairs,
light through the windows—seem foreign.
We're back but not back all the way.
Maybe some odd thing lodged in our senses,
some old world cinder
that makes us see things this way,
off balance and askew.
Or maybe just coming back makes us
re-see what we thought we knew so well
we gladly left it behind—
like old friends who know so much about us

we turn them into strangers.
We left all this, hoping it would hold together,
keeping old worries hostage in the attic
while we gamboled in our elsewhere.
It tried hard but we guess
the effort forced these changes
just because we branched out toward
the green possibles of that other life.
Now we've lost that life
and can't quite find the old one,
back here where sidewalk cracks veer in ways
we can't read. And there's a vase
we don't recognize, a room turned wrong way round,
a cup looking left-handed.
An accent not quite American,
not quite anything else, hovers here.
We hear it at dinner as we hold this strange silverware,
its points of balance oddly shifted,
its odd shapes changing the shapes of our fingers
and giving the food flavors
we've never tasted before.

Learning Your Lesson

The first time you choke it down,
gagging all the way,

your throat remembering the texture
for days.

Later you grow immune
to the flavor of your pride

and chugalug it
time after time

like everyone else
who has acquired the taste.

Reclaiming the House

It confirms our dreams—all year
it circled there, waiting, harboring
so much of us we travelled light
with thanks. Now that life floods back
with a steady throb all night
and we learn it all again slowly,
the way we work through all
the accumulated mail, the stacks
of magazines that give lost time
a shape.
       We are the creatures
of this place—when it worries
over high winds we worry, too,
unlike last year in someone else's
house where we didn't really have
to worry when something went on
the fritz.
       Here we wait for Fritz
and know how he plans his small
betrayals—the disposal choking
on a bone, the refrigerator running
a fever, the cellar letting in
rain through all its pores.
You know you're home when a whining
hinge makes you wince and you
feel tortured by a dripping
faucet. It is *our* faucet!
It should know better!

But it doesn't,
any more than a broken table does
or the dishes gone to their reward
in our absence do. The connection runs
deep, nearly metaphysical, and when
something is on the blink we search
for someone else to blame but know
that no matter how we try there is
no one else to blame but ourselves.

Driving North

Going up 101 we let each scene
die behind each curve,
our eyes hungry
for what comes next

like a book you can't put down.
But the detail is too rich—
we take in what we can,
water walking away with

pieces of sky on its back,
three spindly trees poking
bony branches akimbo
like signposts for the anorexic.

Which says nothing of the Pacific
basking out there or, far inland,
those white acres of sand
sprouting unlikely pines.

The world never edits, says:
*Here, take it all at once
in one gulp.* Our eyes, trained
for pictures, try to pick and choose,

emend this sight, add flourishes
to that, yet it never quite
works out and we wind up
letting the car's speed

blue pencil much of what we pass.
But because we are together
we feel we've somehow got it all,
scooped up and put on file—

the stop in Cloverdale,
that lunch in Cannon Beach.
And when we get home we'll
add it up just to make sure.

Keeping It Together

For a start you use
tea and talk, the day's
first dark headlines
and your dreams go
numb—that looming face
pretending to be a ripe
harvest moon stands still,
then fades to a dot
like a TV turned off.
Next your delicacy gathers
in the eggs you carry
to the stove—the shells
are so thin these days,
they break into
such small pieces.
You drive over those pieces
to the delights of key,
office, mail and the heady
vertigo buried in
the heart of grammar.
(O be with me now,
muse of the comma splice!)
Such rich incident carries
you to three, though the clock
is so hesitant, pausing so long
as if holding its breath
before its nervous leap forward.

And finally the omens:
Scrawny birds on that
skimpy tree out your window,
the exit marked Graceless,
and rain whispering
its million run-on sentences.

Spending the Night

The plank bridge rumbles—
I hold my breath
to get our roadster
                    all the way across,
my father swearing
and shifting to low,
                    planks drumming
hard and—miracle!—
                    we're safe,
steering the grandfather ruts
past the barn no one
had the heart to finish—
ragged two-by-fours
pointing toward the sky
like broken promises.
                    I feel
flannel sheets
and swooping rafters
dreaming me alone and lost
as the kitchen door invents
her silhouette.
                    My parents
leave me there
                    and I breathe
the ether taste of losing them
in some dark crease
                    of the night,
the roadster gunning back across

the flimsy bridge toward their dance.
I try to follow them
but dusk swallows their car
beyond the road's first curve.
Quickly her slippers stroke
irritable whispers
across the floor,

              chunks of pine
clang angrily in the stove.
She loves noise and wants
her kettle to scream
really loud before she lifts it
from the burner.
My elbows on the table,
I stare into the dull mirror
of a spoon,

          my face blurred
and moony as a tired ghost,
features rubbed thick
and useless.

            She seems angry
as she always does at first
and I remember my mother
saying: *Pay no attention
to her stories.*

           They're just stories.
She still seems testy
when she gives me the milk
and cookies I hate,

           bits of cream
floating in the glass,

              suspicious raisins
lurking in the cookies.
                 But I play the game
pretending to like them
as she pretends that I want more.
I barely nibble at the extra cookie,
ignore the ugly milk
              then she swoops
plate and glass away saying
what a finicky eater I am.
It's always a bad bargain
between us—
          she the famous cook
and me the child who hates food.
For her I'm not quite human,
refusing to be her glutton.
At the sink she washes
and mutters.
         I trace the pattern
on the oilcloth.
         Her kitchen
is always too hot,
         hotter
when she's in it,
         adding her anger
to the steam.
         She cheers up though
and says it's time
for *Lights Out* on the radio.
With the lights out
         the cat's eye

of the dial winks green
and I pretend to listen
while thinking myself across
the room and carefully
out the window
the way I learned
to work it at the dentist's.
Looking in now
                    I see her
roll a cigarette
                    pulling
the Bull Durham string
tight with her teeth
                    like a cowboy.
She leans forward as she listens,
darting glances at the chair
where she thinks I sit
                    but I keep roaming
the chill air
                    around the house.
I come back in—
                    she's mad
because I didn't cringe even
once during the program.
A bad show tonight, she says,
nothing like *The Chicken Heart*
or *Donovan's Brain.*
I laugh and say it was scary
enough for me,
                    faking a shudder
and she smiles

but warily
and I worry about my fake shudder.
Then like the good counterpuncher
she is, she starts my bedtime story
before I can think myself away—
It's just a story
                    my mother's voice
whispers from the dance
                              Just a story—
but it's too late,
                    the dance hall
too far away.
                    She tells me about a boy
pulled bloated and ugly
from the creek,
                    all his features
just rinsed away,
                    the poor little tyke's
throat slit ear to ear
                    poor pitiful
little thing
                    and just your age, too.
I try not to wince but feel the skin
on my throat tense and taste
the way she said "rinsed"
and all at once remember
                              my moony face
in the spoon
                    features blurred
out of shape. There is always a story
I can't quite think away—

she always finds the images
that loom in the mind
                              no matter how
I try to squint them away.
They dangle in the dark like bats
or creatures worse than bats,
worse even than my own
                              nightmare tigers
caught in my pillow at home.
I listen for my mother's voice
but it's gone.
                    It's very dark
in the attic room
                    and the smells come
back, wood and dust,
a dampness like old newspapers
and her trunk is there
where she finds the images
she dangles in the darkness
from that mixture of sachet
and camphor
                    and old lace
brittle as dead leaves, ribbons
faded colorless,
                    her wedding dress
yellow and streaked.
                         I try flying
out the window
                    but the flannel sheets
hold me back.
                    The room grows large,

corners yawning toward caverns,
floor tilting
          to let my bed
slide down oily chutes,
                 walls falling away
toward icy nakedness.
I try to fly again but think
only of the boy with his features
rinsed away.
        I rub my face to find
my features and think they feel okay.
Now something feathery and dusty
brushes my cheek,
then the bottom of the night
drops away
        and I fall through
the plank bridge into the cold
dark water of forever.

Learning to Draw

When he drew I wanted to wear
his hand like a glove,
my fingers inside his.
I squinted hard, made a fist,
whittled myself down
to the tip of his pencil, feeling
the curves, the shading,
those curlicue breathtaking
journeys up and around. I longed
for the speed of his lines
spiraling across the nickel
tablet as if they were finding
their way out of a maze
and making the maze, too.
I laughed when a face appeared—
complete, grinning, lifted
out of that dull pond of paper,
hooked by the pencil's tip.
I needed to get inside
the glove of his hand,
my small fingers fitting
easily beside the big callus
on his middle finger, eager
to make that intricate journey,
avid to turn the tablet's cheap
paper into mystery, into pictures
like an icing on the world,
like answers to the echoing

questions the night asked—
distant howls, the owl's
deep who's, those skittering
feet inside my dreams.
At first the pencil threw
a fit between my fingers, lines
going everywhere but right.
Keeping at it for months,
I finally felt the first nudge
of a callus that I rubbed
for luck every time
I picked the pencil up.

Killing Time

Our laziness makes such demands
we're already exhausted by noon

with the whole rest of the day
to wade through. What do we do?

The sun so bright, the clock so
crammed with hours?

We rummage for that list we once
made, we try memories

but they crawl toward us like slugs,
each uglier than the last.

The sun moves so slowly!
Evening is so far away!

If we could kill time we would
but where is its neck? Its heart?

O Baudelaire, we long for the ecstasy
of your ennui! For us only this

vacancy we stare into, this shallow
abyss with no eyes of its own,

this place where every clock
is the one that never moved

in grade school. And we know
when it finally strikes three

no release will come, no racing
across the schoolyard with coats

flying. For our laziness the teacher
will keep us after school forever.

Calling Up the Pain

Then the day came when we called
and it didn't answer. We were
far away in an exile interior
and otherwise, living in a town
called Brown Study located
in The Middle Distance. We chose it
for its nearness to Forgetfulness
and the scarcity of telephones.
We put our lives on hold.
We turned off the answering
service far back in the brain.
But that day came. It was like
probing a bruise and finding
all the blue had drained away;
even the last of the yellow
with its echo of true pain
was gone. For a time we missed it,
longing briefly for the edge
it gave our days. For a time we
sought it out working a kind of awkward
carpentry, building from memory,
our thick fingers all thumbs.
What we came up with was half
guesswork, half textbook vending
machine. When we put in our wooden
nickels something like pain
came out but it tasted of
saccharin and preservatives—

to our great relief. We had hoped
true pain in the right circumstances
was biodegradable. We had looked
long and hard for the right
circumstances. We called again
and got a busy signal, again
and the phone was disconnected.
We didn't rejoice exactly
and still kept testing the spot
where the bruise had been.

Taking the Old Road

Yesterday we fell for it again,
letting ourselves be herded
along I-5—all traffic
a single-minded seventy, roadsides
like blinders, farmland and towns
turned into vague rumors.
Today we wanted no more of being told
there was only one way to go
but had to ask three times
for the old road—no one seemed to remember.
Their directions took us into hills,
along roads with aliases and alibis
and no true identities.
We had their meaning—anything off
the freeway is an illusion,
those roads and towns edited out of memory,
but finally an old man
killing time on a corner understood
and sent us free of cloverleafs and ramps.
The traffic thinned and we drove
into our own past, through towns
with real names—Woodburn, Aurora, Canby.
Suddenly a local version of the world appeared—
people on sidewalks, schools, houses,
and our eyes filled as we slowed
to a human speed passing landmarks
like the Chuckhole Tavern,
Antique Buffaloes, and Flo's Beauty Salon

and Ferry. We knew again how interstates
were meant to drain wit away
with their simple numbers.
And for us the map came alive
and Main Streets bounced into view
like those remembered from childhood,
dreaming by in evening light
with those mysterious lives of strangers
hovering under streetlamps,
people we would never know.
Freeways pound travel to amnesia
the way airports do—duplicates of each other,
history carefully washed away,
a method for losing the past—those towns,
those farms we came from
as if they were guilty secrets.
But for miles we were back there
travelling the old two-lanes in ancient heavy cars,
our parents talking quietly in the front seat,
as we counted livestock
in misty pastures and wondered
about the people wool-gathering behind those
single lighted windows in all the lonely farmhouses.

Moon Driving

We expect the night to fool us
but it doesn't. It stays dark.

The moon flips its lethargic coin.
We yawn. Trees sleep

and traffic falls off the edge
of town for all we know.

We follow some with our
lights off, letting

the moon do the driving.
Most of the cars only go home

like dogs in boring stories.
Only a few fall off.

But we're out there now
running roads in the dark,

chased by the night's scolding tongue
like a long-dead teacher,

the one we called the Nazi.
It's good to be out here,

hearing our tires mate with the tar,
seeing the tar unroll just at our speed.

This is what we were meant to do—
drive all night and keep the trees awake.

Disappearing

Something like snow covers you
Something like white water

Your breath becomes this strangeness
You mix with it like dye

Later someone finds your name
On a table at Goodwill

Almost like new almost a perfect fit
It strikes his fancy and the price is right

He takes it home
And your family greets him warmly

Calling him by name kissing him
Saying oh how it suits you

Remaking Yourself

First you travel back
Tracing canals
Wandering old wheatfields
Until you
Trap the seed
Fence it in
And make it confess its code
This takes time of course
Most seeds are stubborn
And very proud
They call themselves winners
They expect nothing less
Than the uebermensch
And you've been a grave disappointment
Eventually though
Yours will come across
Opening his thick skin
Along the hidden zipper
Then you must revise his code quickly
Muddling the Xs and Ys
Or whatever they are
Until they form the recipe you want
After this you need patience
Waiting for the sprouts the hopes
The tendrils like question marks
The new disappointments coiled
Like unexposed film

Missing It

Over the tall maples,
along gutters strewn
with old gold
and the maniacal
gardener's sprinkler
water, past the idiot
stumps of two birches
lopped off by the new
arrivals, deep into
the summer-soft
tar of the street—
windows rumbled
nervous by passing
buses—it comes
and we pay no
attention like
the deaf in an air
raid, the blind
lazily turning their
opaque eyes to
the sun; it comes
near sleep with
a name like the tic
in a tired eyelid,
then we pass with it
into sleep's soft
ebony without writing

it down and the maples
go on and on with their
cheap sentimental
gossip about it
until it sleeps too.

Killing Flies in Georgia

I go only part way back tonight,
sidetracked by fly buzz and the lies
of old letters, and then Blotchy
starts killing flies again and all
the years between do their crumbling
act, off-stage voices whispering cues
I can't quite catch—wind and rivers,
dead time plucking corroded wires.
The light changes and we're in that
town again, faces out of focus
in the background, name tags on
their fatigues blurred fuzzy, the ink
running.
            But we're free of Sergeant
Sanchez for a sweet forty-eight
and start carefully with dinner, wanting
at least an acre of white tablecloth,
wanting china plates and waitresses
calling us honey. Silver kissing china
is the sound we float in, letting
our voices dye that liquid gently.
Now we are in the bar, lights wavery
as underwater light, ashtrays like
seashells, Carpenter saying it looks
like everybody's senior prom. But we
like the taste of ocean here, the tacky
decorations, a boat lashed to the ceiling
seeming to bob and drift in that watery

gloom. I think of our cadre up there
fishing for us, hooks aimed at our
eyes, Sergeant Sanchez grinning
his evil grin.

            Carpenter seems drunk
already but you never know with him,
he likes to pretend. Soon he's telling us
Johnny Cash is his second cousin
and wrote "I Walk the Line" plunked
down in his parents' house. Bullshit,
Blotchy says, two pink spots the size
of quarters on his cheeks. No, man,
Carpenter says, He sure as hell did,
right there on that red vinyl couch.
But you ain't no cracker, Blotchy yells.
Neither is Johnny, Carpenter winks,
fishing the news out with a smirk.
His real name's Mario Antonelli
and he went to the New York High
School of Performing Arts with my uncle,
Tex Ritter. Bullshit, Blotchy mutters.
Bullshit.

            Carpenter's stories come back
on a breeze, edited by fly buzz
and the look of old letters, ink
unsure of itself, the crease of the folds
like scars.

            With each round the barracks
floats farther away, our bunks like rafts.
Tony is quiet, growling curses against
the army, his pachuco mark beginning

to shine like a ragged jewel on his
forehead.

A black trio sings "Mary
Anne," then a man called Graveyard—
"Because I'm so damn old"—sings
gravelly blues.

Every watching face
is white neon around us and I
remember the ratty cord
at the bus station dividing people
by color. Now Carpenter says he
went to prep school with Bing Crosby's
kids. Real pricks, he says. Blotchy
doesn't bother to comment, coughing
as if his one good lung is pulling
loose, one cough at a time.

With all
the seashells and nets, the boat trolling
above us, we ask for twists of minnow
in our drinks, tiny goldfish in
the fancy ones. The bartender doesn't
smile. We go on swimming through
the night and faces from our platoon
rise from the surf and sink away
after elaborate long-lost greetings.
Carpenter is talking about his days
in Paris with Scott and Zelda, punting
on the Seine, dropping by for hot dogs
with Gertrude and Alice. I join him
at Shakespeare and Company, splitting
a bottle of white wine with Joyce

until we forget and begin arguing
baseball. You guys are plain nuts,
Blotchy yells over the music, cheeks
brick-red half dollars, coughs erupting
after each drag on a Camel.
                              Tony scuttles
in sea-bottom gloom, talking about
Maria in L.A., hating the army,
saying he's on Sanchez's shit list.
Ain't we all, Blotchy says and we
all laugh. Even Tony grins.
                              Suddenly
we are walking and it's raining,
Carpenter singing "I Walk the Line,"
Blotchy trying to join in, croaking
and coughing. Mysteriously, we're now
far away from the clip joints walking
under shade trees among huge white
houses. We take in the silence with care,
that taste of houses and families,
but they move ages away quickly,
the army screening us out, moving
invisibly to deny us the world,
reading our mail before it's written.
Then the ruin turns up: On the gate
a plaque says it was a military
academy closed for good in 1861,
kept on as a monument. Soft moss
smothers the crumbling stone and I
think of the last crazy class riding
out to die in Pickett's charge. I think

of the ratty cord, too.
                    All the years
between crumble, too, and that night
is here with Carpenter's fancy lies
and Blotchy's cough, Tony cursing
and longing for Maria, the pachuco
mark darkening as the night wears out.
Givens is somehow with us, too,
Sanchez's scapegoat—he hovers above us.
Barracks rumor said he tried to
hang himself in the boiler room—
no one knows for sure but Givens
was gone, footlocker and uniforms,
mattress rolled up like a snail,
cot springs echoing.
                    Tony is saying,
No way, man, no way. Ain't going
to be no Givens. I ain't going back.
Drinking rum from a coke bottle,
we argue with him but then forget,
back drifting in that ceiling boat
beyond all sergeants. Then Blotchy
loses his cap but comes back with
a new one he steals from a GI
drunker than he is. It's far too
small, perching on his head like
a beany and we laugh over this
far too long.
                    Tony keeps calling
for Maria and we feel helpless
to do anything but go AWOL

with him forever. The idea charms us.
I see the hill we'll go over,
richly green and soft, the other side
like Shangri-la. But we lose track
again, laughing over Blotchy's tiny
cap.
    Now we're in the hotel
with Blotchy killing flies, hitting
the wall with the heel of his fist.
Each time his hand looks bloodier
but the flies never move. He keeps
pounding and looking puzzled, red
dollars on his cheeks flaming.
Bastards won't die, he yells.
Tony struggles up with his rum bottle
and squints at the wall, teetering.
Then his eyes widen. Christ, man, those
ain't flies, those're nails, army's
driving you nuts. Blotchy stares
at his ragged hand and begins laughing
and coughing his terrible cough.
Then we all laugh, the room too small
to hold it all. You ignorant private
E-nothing, Carpenter squeaks,
rolling off the bed and we laugh on
and on and the whole lost night,
our whole lives, come to rest on that
wall smeared with Blotchy's drunken
blood.
    So much takes place off-stage,
everything a confusion of rumors:

Blotchy court-martialed in Munich
for pistol-whipping a young lieutenant,
Carpenter in market research stealing
our souls, Tony in one story putting
his foot on a train track in Korea,
finally getting back to Maria.
In fly buzz I hear Blotchy's terrible
cough and Carpenter's hilarious lies
veering away into an endless sky.
I see Tony limping alone along
an L.A. street and those nailheads
jutting out and all of us laughing.

Listening to a Russian Choir

The voices sing
                    of long avenues
                                    inside stones,
of distances so
                vast you've
                            run out of miles
to count them with.
                    The voices say follow
                                    if you can
keep up, stay warm,
                    our winter has no end.
                                    Forget all those
hours lost with
                your cold hands
                                folded, obeying some
teacher's bilious frown.
                        We promise you'll never
                                        have to color between
the lines again
                or ask permission
                                to leave a room.
So scribble your
                straight and narrow
                                    fat and crooked—
we couldn't care less.
                    Let parts of speech
                                    change places like

partners at a dance—

                         choose St. Vitus

                                     if you want—he's good.

These songs mean

                    business. They plant

                              the itch to fly

deep in your shoulders,

                      hint at your latent talent

                                    for wings

and love to slip the noose

                      of language, letting

                                nouns and verbs

disagree whenever they

                    like, begging commas

                                to swim off like manic

tadpoles. The voices

                    rise and fall, tease,

                              caress. They keen

all edges smooth,

                    rough up

                    your pantywaist

nostalgia just for

                    fun or swarm like

                            fire looping up

a flue, then swirl

                    with the spit and hiss

                            of downed wires

spilling their sap.

                  Keep up if you can,

                      stay warm, the journey

is longer than our
winter that has no end.
See the cathedrals
we build so easily
with our music, see
how easily we topple
them like children's
blocks. We can build
more any time we please.
These songs won't
let you add up
your life's days
with the dull sonnets
of cashier's slips—
they know the toothache
in the hearts of lettuce,
the tragic lives
of artichokes,
the dark insomnia
of potatoes
and semolina's migraines.
But pay no attention—
make bouquets of all
your loose ends
and mail them
to the sandman—
you have no more
need for sleep,
that abandoned factory.
Forget the backing and filling

of dependent clauses,
                 let the periodic sentence
                                  die of natural
causes. They say dive off
                 the deep end, let
                            your dry wit drown
and free yourself
                 of the tyranny of keys
                            and better mousetraps.
We know a secret
                 inoculation against
                         the law of gravity
and we'll make damn sure
                 all your enemies' boats
                           pound to kindling
on the rocks—this is only
                 one of many fringe benefits.
                            So fly with us and
                            call
all the Milky Way's
                 unlisted numbers
                     one by one
while soaring in our
                 troika and throwing
                       caviar to the wolves.

Getting Out of the Army

for Joan

Those last few months I was edgy
        having saluted one officer too many,
sure I would wind up saying the wrong
        thing and lose my soft-touch job

and early release or even worse—
        they're always tough on short-timers.
It was then you started buying back
        my childhood and I put together

model after model of the hero planes
        I loved in 'forty-three and four.
Mustangs, those slim cigars with their
        elegant bubble cockpits, workhorse

Hellcats built like stocky guards
        and catchers, lovely gull-winged
Corsairs and that era's Toyota—the Zero.
        I was a factory living through

that war again turning out aircraft
        and back in California, scanning
the horizon for Mitsubishi bombers
        as the swaybacked PBYs

lumbered out to sea on patrol.
        My Spitfires and Hurricanes saved

Britain from the Blitz one more time
    and I traveled nights with

the mysterious Black Widows like
    catamarans, the night fighters
of all our dreams. I felt all their controls
    in my hands and spiraled with

vertigo down with the newsreels'
    fishtailing bombs from Flying
Fortresses and Liberators, flew B-25s
    with Doolittle from carriers to bomb

Tokyo in 'forty-two. I fought the old war
    smelling balsa wood and glue, those
planes the purest forms of beauty I had
    ever seen. Even the Messerschmitts like

blunt-nose sharks, those graceful
    Focke-Wulfs and the nightmare
scarecrow Stukas screeching down
    on Poland. I worked furiously, model

after model, flying each one as fast
    as you could buy them through those last
tense months, managing a "sir" when I
    had to, saluting often enough

to stay out of hot water before I flew
    free for good when I threw my
cap in the sky over Fort Hamilton
    and we watched, knowing it would fly.

Camping with Ecclesiastes

Pushed to this left-hand corner
of the map we test the dark
for flaws, listening hard
to its thousand versions of silence
working their slow way
through the trees
leaf by leaf.
We're a long way from the Continental
Divide's big news but we don't care.
Our rivers flow the other way—
so what if all the others meander east
where it's already morning,
our eastern doppelgangers
already applying the grindstones
to their noses. Will their early birds
get all the worms? Probably.
They usually do.
But if they have such appetites
we'll concede them all the worms
they can eat—keeping only the fattest
for our fish. They seem to like the
flavor
and it's the least we can do
as their numbers dwindle
toward zero, our rivers running fevers.
And we have other bleak omens:
Buzz saws clearcutting hills,
oily rags of gulls trembling

on our beaches.
Death is no respecter of time zones.
Here at least we know the abyss
is within easy driving distance—
we can hear its bored yawn
if we listen closely.
Once our rivers ran so thick with fish
our horses shied, afraid to ford
such torrents of teeth.
Now only the toughest or luckiest
salmon makes it and the rivers
go on pouring themselves
into the sea that's never full
and we go camping with Ecclesiastes,
that cynical old trapper.
He knows the words to every camp song
ever written and makes fun of each one we sing.
What about a stirring round
about entropy? he roars, laughing,
then asks if we really like it here.
We can't just say yes—in spite of clearcuts
and dead fish it still runs deeper
than like; it's not some simple flesh wound
or vanity. Our world begins with our skin
and carries on out to a sky
too wide to wear with any comfort—
and yes, like everyone else's
it's often salted with particulates of greed.
Some days we chew it,
some days it gnaws our vision raw.
But with the abyss just a hop and a skip away

we tolerate the hopeless air,
even find a few pure pockets
if we walk far enough,
ignoring the old trapper's sarcastic snorts.
We remember late nights
when the rain ran clear, washing windows clean.
And how our mothers
caught it in barrels to rinse their hair.

Travelling One Way

Sit and listen
               the little towns
call you
         with their dinky stores
and their young evaporating
in summer heat
              between
the angled cars
            moth-wish
and murder mingling some
strangled milkshake
of speed and lassitude
in their blood
            Listen hard
and aim toward
             those towns
the freeway sidesteps
to make them feel bad
about themselves
              Your town is
there somewhere
              lost in the maps'
crazy folds
But don't push it
Go town by town
Gather each lost street
in your skimpy harvest
              all those
secret people

                    the ghosts you're sure
you know
                before they disappear
squeezed
                to snapshot size
by the rearview mirror
Hear the buzz all things once had
fence wires taut
as banjo strings
                        Your town
can't have learned a disguise
good enough to fool you
You know
                    every sidewalk crack
that squinting
                    angle of the sun
blaring across the lake
that lapping sound
                        of water
that pulls a memory
part way out
                    then snaps it twanging
back
        skimming the midnight
moontrack toward oblivion
Tonight
            you need the right
names on the right corner
the dog that knows you
and that thin
                volcanic air
that lets you breathe

                        again
Pay no attention
to the bum steers
                  the rich
dark gives you
                  counting its money
And if you play it right
other late ghosts
will turn up
                  paper thin
jogging the road's shoulder
They'll lead you
Call them by name
                        tamarack
fir
   jackpine
            Like whispering
road signs they'll
                  guide you
past moth-wish and murder
along that last sure path
held in place
                  by moon-spattered
lashes of leaves
Just through there your
town waits
            the right names
gathered on the corner
the good dog that knows you
and that ozone air
that teaches you
how to breathe again

About the Author

A native of the Pacific Northwest, Vern Rutsala received his B.A. from Reed College and his M.F.A. from the University of Iowa. He is the author of numerous poetry books. His previous book, *The Moment's Equation,* was a finalist for the National Book Award in poetry. Among his awards are a Guggenheim fellowship, two National Endowment for the Arts fellowships, the Richard Snyder Prize, and the Kenneth O. Hanson Award. Rutsala taught at Lewis & Clark College from 1961-2004.